CLARA'S MAGIC GARDEN

Florin T. Kolbaba

Scott J. Kolbaba, MD

ILLUSTRATED BY DINA LEUCHOVIUS

Online Publishers
ClarasMagicGardenBook.com

Clara's Magic Garden
Published by Online Publishers
ClarasMagicGardenBook.com

ISBN (hardcover) 979-8-9884016-0-5
ISBN (paperback) 979-8-9884016-1-2
ISBN (e-book) 979-8-9884016-2-9
LCCN: 2023909706

Edited by Deborah K. Frontiera,*www.authorsden.com/deborahkfrontiera*
Illustrations by Dina Leuchovius, *www.stayinmay.online*
Design by Monica Thomas for TLC Book Design, *TLCBookDesign.com*

To the twelve grandchildren who make our lives rich:

Danika, Zoey, Cameron, Elyssa, Quinn, Wyatt,
Grayden, Avery, Olivia, Aiden, Claire, and Marley.

And to those who have felt like little Clara and the bush,
may you find your purpose.

We would like to express our appreciation to those who helped make this book possible. First to Joan, my wife and Florin's mother, who served as our first editor. When she said, "this is not good enough," she was always right. Ellyse Wetzker was our model for little Clara. She is as beautiful as Clara because she has learned her true worth from nurturing parents, Cheryl and Benson, who made a cameo appearance in the book.

We would also like to recognize mother nature for the wise old walnut, the magnolia, the daffodils and the bluebells that really live in our garden beyond our bubbling spring creek. And lastly, the bush, proudly guarding the garden entrance and inspiring us because it really does become the most beautiful thing in the garden.

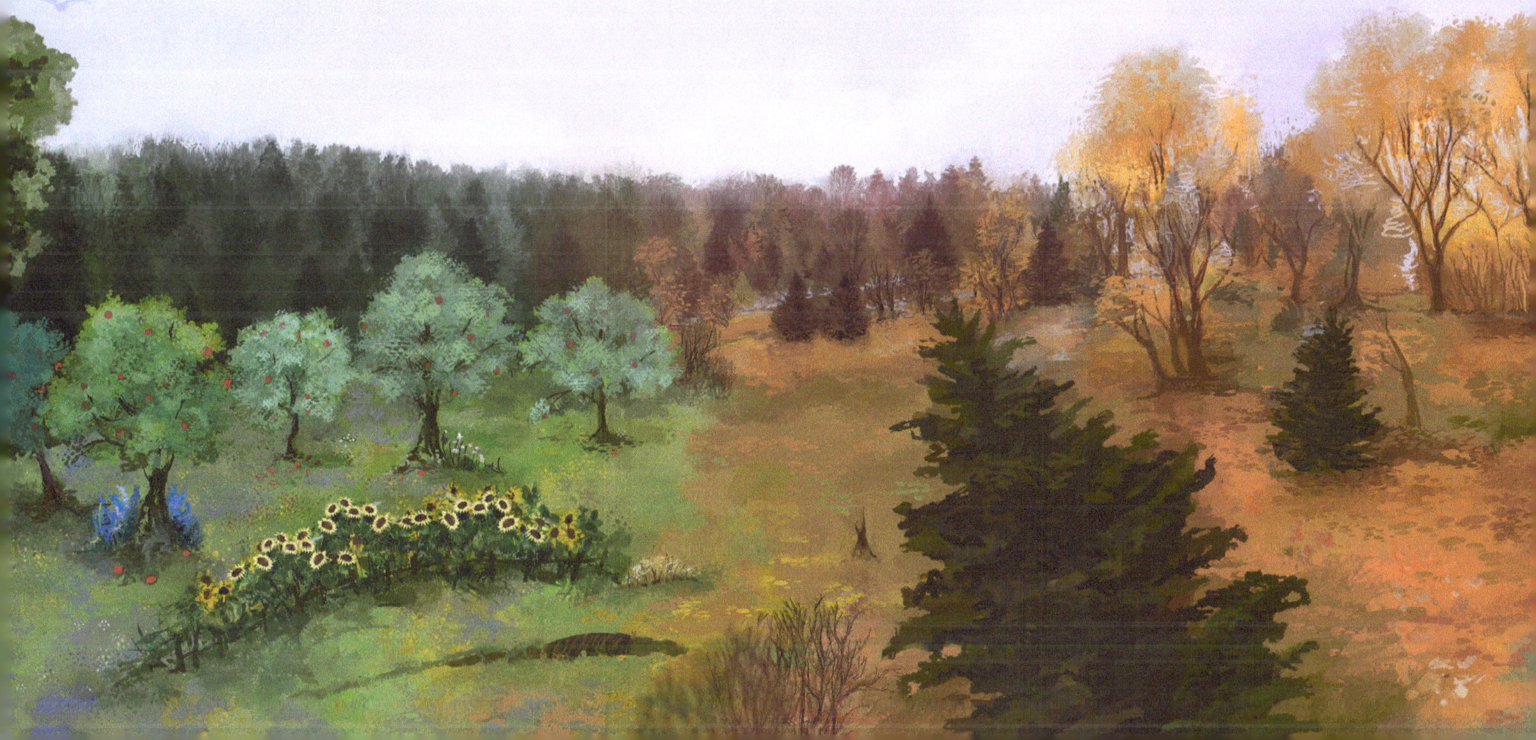

Clara walked through the quiet winter woods alone.
A strange rustling caught her attention.
She followed the sound until she came
across a snow-covered bush.

Clara couldn't believe it!
The bush was actually whispering to her,
and its bright red berries were scattered in the snow.

"They must be magical,"
she thought and picked them up.
"I'll put them in my special collection box
until I can plant them in my garden."

When spring came, she hurried across the wooden bridge
over the bubbling creek that marked the edge
of her hidden garden.

Her friends, a giant walnut tree,
a pink magnolia, yellow daffodils,
and tiny bluebells, lived there.
These were her only friends, and
the garden was her special place.

She decided to plant the berries
under the great shadow of her beloved
walnut at the garden's entrance.
Each round red berry was carefully
placed in a shallow hole in the
soft spring earth.

Every day, before school, she skipped
over the bridge with her watering can
to give the berries a drink.

THEN ONE DAY, IT HAPPENED!

A green sprout peeked its head out of the ground.
Thin branches covered with miniature leaves stretched out,
and it soon became a tiny round bush.

Clara was excited about her new friend,
but the other plants in the garden
did not share her joy.

"Where are its flowers?" asked the daffodils.
"Flowers like ours would look much nicer."

The bush felt unwanted and wondered
if the daffodils could be right.

The next day it reached out
to the magnolia, covered with
colorful pink and white blossoms.

"Will I ever be as pretty as you?"
the bush asked shyly.

"Bush," said the magnolia,
"You are just too plain."

As tears began to well up, their talk was interrupted
by a booming deep voice. It was the walnut, old and wise,
towering over everything in the garden.

"Little bush, I have lived
long and learned much.
Be patient and someday
YOU WILL KNOW
YOUR PURPOSE."

Those were the last
words spoken that day.

The next morning the bush was greeted by
the little girl. Shining drops of dew-tears covered
its green leaves. Clara knew about sadness,
so she lovingly hugged the bush to comfort it.

Summer came to the garden, and Clara walked
out one warm evening to sit on the bridge.

"Little bush," she said, "I know how you feel.
I don't have many friends either."

The bush understood her feelings and
wished it could show her how special she really was.
They had become good friends, and loved each other,
as much as a girl and a bush could.

Time passed, days grew shorter,
and a morning chill filled the air.
The flowers were wilting and
only talking in whispers.
Some stopped talking altogether.

The bush was changing too.
Green leaves turned colors.
"This must be my end," it thought.
"Soon I will not see the sunrise or feel
the gentle rain. I will miss the girl.
She is my only friend."

It recalled the words of the walnut.
"Be patient, little bush, and someday
you will know your purpose."

"But it's too late,"
the bush thought to itself.
"I never really had
a purpose."

Sounds from the house interrupted the chilly
fall morning. Suddenly it saw Clara
running as fast as she could toward it.
Mother and Father followed.

"Look," she yelled.
"Do you see it?
IT'S BEAUTIFUL!"

The bush wondered
what they could be seeing.

Quiet little Clara was actually giggling with joy
because the bush's green leaves had turned to
a brilliant red like a handsome soldier dressed in a
crimson uniform guarding the entrance to the garden.

"I didn't know the berries you planted were from a burning bush that changes colors in the fall," said her mother.

"IT'S THE PRETTIEST THING IN THE GARDEN."

From that day forward, no one ever called the bush plain,
and for the first time Clara was beaming.

And the bush?
Maybe it really did have a purpose—
bringing joy and happiness to a little girl.

Years passed...

Clara grew up, married, and moved away.
She now had children of her own.

But one year, in the fall,
she came back to her magical garden,
to say hello to an old friend,
and to tell her children her story—

how an unhappy little bush
and an unhappy little girl,
who loved each other, grew up together
knowing how special they really were.

On their way home,
Clara's daughter asked her mother
why she called it her magic garden.

"When I was your age," Clara explained,
"I could hear the bush speaking, and it was magical,
but when I was older, I could not hear it anymore," she said sadly.

After her daughter fell asleep,
Clara found a picture that she had
colored on their way home.
It was the bush with tears on its leaves
and the words that only her
daughter could hear...

GOODBYE,
Little CLARA
I LOVE YOU!

ABOUT THE AUTHORS

Scott J. Kolbaba, MD, has been a practicing physician for longer than he cares to admit. His first book, *Physicians' Untold Stories,* has been an Amazon bestseller. *Clara's Magic Garden* represents a two-year culmination of work with his son, Florin. Dr. Kolbaba's greatest joy comes from his family of seven children. On their yearly vacations they love to launch the largest kites on the beach and frequent as many ice cream shops as possible.

Florin T. Kolbaba was excited to collaborate with his father on their first children's picture book. His artful backyard photography formed the basis for the book's paintings. After his experience in writing and marketing, he is planning a consulting business for other aspiring authors. He considers himself a baseball junkie and can name the stats of nearly every player in the major leagues.

ABOUT THE ILLUSTRATOR

Dina Leuchovius is a self-taught artist and illustrator from Sweden. Through her experience writing and illustrating her own book, she found her niche in storybook illustration. When the Kolbaba's saw a sample of her work they knew right away that she would be perfect, and she far exceeded their expectations. This will be her first of many books published in the United States.

www.ingramcontent.com/pod-product-compliance
Lightning Source LLC
Chambersburg PA
CBHW041630110726
48005CB00002B/553